GW00601354

project
~ ONE CORINTHIANS

Written by **Brian Parfitt**

Design by **Catherine Jackson**

Published by CPAS
Adult Training & Resources Unit
Athena Drive
Tachbrook Park
WARWICK
CV34 6NG
Tel: (01926) 334242

ISBN 1 8976 6044 8

Church Pastoral Aid Society
Registered Charity No 1007820
A company limited by guarantee

Group Bible study falls very readily into the trap of not being earthed in reality. It is easy to talk theoretically without looking at the real relevance of a passage for us today. One way to avoid that danger is to use Role Play or Case Studies to highlight the immediate relevance of the topic under discussion. We have chosen this as one of the approaches you can use in Project 1 Corinthians. The fictional parish of St Saviour's has been used to raise issues which arise in many churches from time to time. The goings on at St Saviour's highlight problems the church faces today but they are nothing new. The church in Corinth faced similar issues, even if some of the details have changed a little. This letter has some real challenges for the church as it lives out its life in a society which has much in common with that of Corinth. Our hope is that Project 1 Corinthians will help Christians address those issues today.

Contents

1 ### Growing Together   page 8
AIM To see that Christian maturity is displayed not in division but in unity.
1 Corinthians 1:1-16 & 3:1 - 4:21

2 ### Preaching Christ Crucified   page 12
AIM To see how the message of the cross meets our need of forgiveness and new life.
1 Corinthians 1:17 - 2:16

3 ### Upright Behaviour   page 16
AIM To discover the standards of behaviour expected among Christians.
1 Corinthians 5:1 - 6:19

4 ### Faithful for Life   page 20
AIM To see the value of singleness and of faithful marriage relationships.
1 Corinthians 7

5 ### Limited Freedom   page 24
AIM To learn consideration for the needs and thinking of other people.
1 Corinthians 8:1 - 11:1

6 ### Orderly Worship   page 28
AIM To value the needs of the whole church, and to appreciate the need for order in
our worship.
1 Corinthians 11:2-33 & 14:20-40

7 ### All Good Gifts   page 32
AIM To discover how to use our gifts for the good of all.
1 Corinthians 12:1 - 14:19

8 ### Faithful to the End   page 36
AIM To see how Christian beliefs shape Christian lives.
1 Corinthians 15 & 16

How do I Use This Book?

It contains a series of eight studies. Within each section you will find:

ON THE FIRST TWO PAGES

 AIM The main point which should emerge from that week's study.

 INTRODUCTION Some general points about the passage as a whole and guidelines on the studies themselves.

 NOTES Explanation of individual verses to give you a fuller understanding of the passage. You may like to read some of these out to the group when it would help.

 SUNDAY EXTRA Ideas for adapting the theme for Sunday Worship either before or after the group meetings. (Suitable hymns are listed in the WORSHIP & PRAYER section).

THE NEXT PAGE IS THE...

GROUP SHEET This may be photocopied. *(Please see details in the copyright note on the title page.)* It has all the basic material for a Bible Study on the week's passage and contains:

 CASE STUDY / ROLE PLAY These are intended to provide a starting point for discussion which earths the themes of 1 Corinthians in the experience of churches today. They are based around events in the life of the fictional St Saviour's. You can use them as a base for role play or you can use the scenes from St Saviour's as Case Studies to raise the issues discussed in 1 Corinthians. If the Case Study seems unrelated to your experience of church life, to give variety you can start your study instead with the BEGIN HERE ALTERNATIVES on the opposite page.

 BIBLE STUDY Questions which help the group to explore the meaning and message of the passage, beginning with a Bible Link question which establishes the connection between the issues raised in the opening discussion and the problems faced by the church in Corinth. The questions on this page aim to bring out the principles of Paul's teaching in the letter.

 APPLICATION Steps to take to apply what has been learned in a practical way.

OPPOSITE, FOR EASY REFERENCE BY THE GROUP LEADER, THERE ARE

 BEGIN HERE ALTERNATIVE Use these as an alternative to the Role Play / Case Study approach to give greater variety or when the Case Study would not be relevant to your group.

 ADDITIONAL QUESTIONS These are more practically related or dig deeper into the text. You can integrate some of these with the questions on the worksheet or work through them separately, especially if you want a study that goes a little deeper. This could be an alternative Bible study to the one on the GROUP SHEET.

WORSHIP & PRAYER Ideas to help the group worship and pray together, including possible hymns and songs. The numbers given are from the popular *Mission Praise* combined edition but most of the songs will be found in other books too. These can be used at the meeting or during Sunday worship.

How Do I Prepare?

1 PREPARE YOURSELF

Pray about the passage, the study, the group and yourself as leader.

Work quickly through the GROUP SHEETS, as if you were an ordinary group member. Jot down notes, questions, and areas to expand or work on. Be honest with yourself and let God teach you as you prepare.

Read through the passage and the notes again. Be guided by the AIM.

2 PLAN YOUR APPROACH

Decide how you are going to tackle the study. There are a number of possible approaches to each passage. You may decide to take two weeks over a study in order to make use of all the material.

The Bible study on the GROUP SHEETS has a helpful explanation of the passage. This can be read aloud to the group or read in silence by the members. The questions which follow are about the way the passage applies to us today. Decide on your approach: you can leave the questions until you have read all the introduction, or you can discuss each question at the point marked in the notes.

You can use the material on the GROUP SHEETS every week. Or, on the principle that 'variety is the spice of life', you can use the ALTERNATIVE METHOD OF STUDY for some of your meetings. This will give you another 'way in' to what the passage says and it can be used in place of the explanation of the passage on the GROUP SHEETS. (Each ALTERNATIVE METHOD offers a different approach; these can be used for looking at other passages in future meetings.) You can also use the ADDITIONAL QUESTIONS to substitute for, or supplement, the questions on the GROUP SHEETS. Make sure you always include BEGIN HERE and ACTION.

3 ASSESS THE TIMING

You will not have time to cover all the material so don't set out thinking this is the aim. Marks will not be deducted if the paper is not completed! You need to use what is appropriate and helpful to your group. Think carefully about the timing of each section. We have not put down suggestions for times, since each group will have different priorities. However we suggest that, as you prepare, you WRITE DOWN your target time for each section.

Try to keep to a basic framework each week and allocate times for prayer, reading, discussion and coffee, even though you may feel a longer prayer time, for example, is appropriate on some occasions. It is good to end promptly so that those who need to do so can go, leaving others to chat if they wish.

Introducing I Corinthians

A society with loose moral standards and with a pride in its intellectual and philosophical achievements; Christians influenced by society's moral attitudes and seeking intellectual acceptability; a church with a variety of doctrinal outlooks, split over charismatic gifts and with divided loyalties to leaders – it all sounds familiar to modern ears, but it is the church in first century Corinth we are describing.

CORINTH

Corinth was on the narrow isthmus, four miles wide, linking southern Greece with the rest of the country and the world beyond. It was a key centre of trade. Travellers on land had to come through it, while sea traffic too crossed the isthmus. (Smaller boats were carried over on rollers, while larger ships transferred their cargoes overland to another boat.) Like most ports it had a reputation for immorality, encouraged by the thousand priestesses of the temple of Aphrodite, goddess of love, who were sacred prostitutes. The temple of Apollo, the ideal of masculine beauty, had its male equivalent of Aphrodite's priestesses.

Corinth was a cosmopolitan place. The original Greek city had been razed to the ground in 146BC in punishment for its part in the revolt of the Greek city states against Roman occupation. It was refounded in 46BC by Julius Caesar as a Roman colony and became the provincial capital. It thus had a core of Roman citizens, but its commercial position meant it soon attracted people of all backgrounds, including a good number of Jews. It became a wealthy city. The Isthmian Games, second only to the Olympic Games, were held there. It was probably one of the toughest places in which to proclaim the gospel! Despite the mixture of races in Corinth, the Greek interest in philosophical thought seems to have shaped the intellectual life of the city. The religious life of Corinth readily adopted foreign gods, many of whose cults offered special insight and ecstatic religious experiences. This too coloured the outlook of the church in Corinth.

PAUL IN CORINTH

We read in Acts 18:1-18 how Paul founded the church in Corinth. He arrived there from Athens, probably in 50AD, without his colleagues Silas and Timothy. He was welcomed by Priscilla and Aquila, Jews who had left Rome because of the persecutions there. Like Paul they were tent makers and he joined them in business. When Silas and Timothy arrived from Macedonia with a gift from the church in Philippi he was able to devote himself entirely to preaching. Initially he met a good response in the synagogue – even Crispus its ruler, was converted. Later opposition led to him preaching in the house next door instead. Paul speaks in 1 Corinthians of his weakness and fear as he preached in Corinth. A dream reassured him that he was doing the right thing and so he spent a year and a half there, despite some opposition when Gallio arrived as the new Consul. Later he moved to Ephesus with Priscilla and Aquila. It was there that Apollos was helped to a full understanding of the faith by Priscilla and Aquila and was sent to preach in Corinth (see Acts 18:24-19:1). Some time later Paul wrote a letter to the Corinthians about avoiding the company of fornicators and this was taken to encourage a total separation from non-Christians, which was not Paul's intention (see 1 Corinthians 5:9). Then people from Chloe's household brought news (1 Corinthians 1:11) and a letter was brought from Corinth by Stephanas, Fortunatus and Achaicus (1 Corinthians 7:1 and 16:17). As a result Paul wrote this letter to address the problems arising there and to answer questions they had asked.

THE MESSAGE OF 1 CORINTHIANS

Paul's letter addressed the situation in Corinth but it still challenges us today. The details may have changed but the problems have not. The outlook of a secular, immoral society still leads to a lowering of Christian standards or a separatist puritanism. The pressures of intellectualism undermine faith in a crucified and risen Christ. An emphasis on spiritual experiences causes division in the church. Paul deals with all these issues in 1 Corinthians. Its message is as relevant now as then. We need to heed its clarion call to hang on to the basics of Christian faith, to be united and to uphold Christian standards of behaviour. It is very much a message for our times.

Acknowledgements

I should like to express my thanks to all who have helped in the production of this latest in the series of Project Bible studies. My wife Janet, who is my part-time secretary, has patiently typed it, making sense of my illegible scribbles. Rory Keegan and other CPAS staff have provided helpful advice. Catherine Jackson has designed it. In addition, I'd like to say a special thank you to the members of St Matthew's, Kingsdown in Bristol who have been members of the house group I have led for the last eight years. They have helped me learn much about leading groups and have sharpened my skills at writing for groups as they have cheerfully used material I have produced. Their encouragement has been a very important support in my work over the years.

Brian Parfitt

Growing Together
1 CORINTHIANS 1:1-16 & 3:1-4:21

AIM To see that Christian maturity is displayed not in division but in unity.

INTRODUCTION

You thought your church had problems? They are nothing compared to those of the congregation in Corinth! It was a flourishing church, with lively worship and spiritual gifts in abundance. Images of a 'perfect' early church vanish, however, as we read of their difficulties. Chief among them was the divisive 'personality contest' they seem to have set up. Groups within the church championed their favourite preacher: Paul their founder; Apollos who probably had a more philosophical approach; Peter who represented an older Jewish tradition. There was also a 'super-spiritual' group claiming loyalty only to Christ! Such divisions still occur with Christians favouring particular leaders or types of teaching. Paul will have nothing to do with factions. He urges the Corinthians to respect all Christian ministers as servants of God, all contributing to church growth, all answerable to God. No one is superior – not even the Corinthians who had the idea that they were spiritually superior to others, even to Paul himself. This week's passages address these issues and challenge us about the sort of unity we display.

BIBLE NOTES

1:1 The only other time a Sosthenes is mentioned in the Bible is in Acts 18:17. He was the man who became ruler of the synagogue in Corinth after Crispus became a Christian. It may be that Sosthenes followed suit. His link with Corinth would explain why he is included here.

1:2 'Saints' and 'sanctified' have the same Greek root meaning: 'set apart' to be God's people.

1:3 'Grace' and 'peace' are variations on the normal Greek and Jewish greetings which have profound Christian content as they tell of God's love for us and its impact on our lives.

1:4-5 Paul begins in his customary way by giving thanks for those to whom he is writing. His thanksgiving here seems to reflect the Corinthians' view of themselves as a people much blessed by God, particularly in the two areas which are brought to the fore later in the letter – speech and knowledge. Gifts of speech include such things as teaching, prophecy, speaking in tongues and the interpretation of tongues. 'Knowledge' refers to a grasp of Christian truth, which is obviously a good thing. However, the Corinthians overvalued the idea of knowledge, seeing it as a new philosophy giving access to divine mysteries. This at times could lead to vague speculation and philosophising.

1:6-7 Spiritual gifts are seen as a confirmation of the gospel message.

1:7-9 The 'revealing' of Christ and the 'day of our Lord' are references to Christ's return. God will keep all his people secure until that day.

1:11 Chloe was head of a household in Corinth, some of whom had visited Paul and told him about the church there.

1:12 We read of Apollos in Acts 18:24-19:1. He was an eloquent speaker and that may have led to some preferring him to Paul. Cephas (Peter) probably never visited Corinth but those with a Jewish background or sympathies probably used his name as a rallying cry. Those who said they were 'for Christ' were probably being 'super-spiritual', thinking themselves above loyalty to earthly leaders.

3:1-4 'The flesh' (our 'carnal' or 'worldly' nature in some translations) describes the old sinful nature which follows solely human ways of thinking and behaving. Divisions are a sign of following the lower nature.

3:5-9 Paul's agricultural picture of himself as the planter and Apollos as the waterer makes the important point that growth is God-given.

3:10-15 Paul changes the picture to that of a house. Its foundation (faith in Christ) is made by one man and built upon by another. When fire sweeps through a building only things made of durable materials survive. Similarly when our works of service are tested on the day of judgement only good things will survive. All a person's works may fail the test, but that person will still emerge intact, because our salvation depends on God's grace, not on any good works we have done. Salvation will not be taken from us even if we have not been particularly good servants.

3:16-17 The church is seen as a temple in which God is present through his Holy Spirit. It can be destroyed by division – a sin which God will take very seriously.

3:21-23 'Everything belongs to Christ; you are Christ's; therefore everything is yours,' is Paul's logic. That includes all, such as Paul and Apollos, who are his servants (see 4:1) and are therefore there to serve them as well.

4:1-5 Paul's pictures his relationship to Christ as that of a trusted servant or steward who is answerable to a master. He insists that he is accountable to Christ alone.

4:6-7 There is a warning here to avoid pride and the dangers of going beyond what is written in Scripture. At the end of the day they were not all that special – every spiritual gift and insight they possessed had been given them by God, so they couldn't really boast about them.

4:8-13 Christ's people share his glory and his Kingship. The Corinthians were rejoicing in that truth, but ignoring the fact that for Christ and for them the pathway to glory is through suffering, as Paul's example makes clear. There is a degree of irony in this section – particularly in verse 10.

4:14-17 Paul had a special love for the Corinthian Christians. Having led them to faith he was their spiritual father. Timothy too had a special place in his affections. Paul had brought him to faith (Acts 16:1-3) and he had worked with him over many years. Timothy often made visits such as the one to the Corinthians mentioned here. Paul takes care to mention that there was no difference between the teaching he wanted them to follow and that which all the other churches followed.

4:18-21 Paul warns that he is coming to exercise discipline and to sort out problems.

SUNDAY EXTRA

For this week you could think about working together for growth (3:1-4) instead of being divided. **Growth** is **1. Given by God (3:5-9) 2. Tested by God (3:10-17).**

For All-age Worship concentrate on 3:10-15. Use a picture of a house in cross-section. It could be built up bit by bit. Talk about the people involved: labourers to dig foundations; bricklayers; plasterers; plumbers; electricians; roofers. All are of equal importance and all must do their work well. Compare this to the church and the parts various people play in its growth.

You could introduce the theme with a sketch about division. There's to be an election for 'Church President'; people make speeches canvassing support for Paul, Peter and Apollos (or for modern fictional equivalents). Alternatively introduce the need to build with the right materials by retelling the story of the Three Little Pigs. Prayers could focus on church leaders and the need for unity and growth.

Choose hymns and songs from those listed in the **Worship & Prayer** section.

Growing Together

1 CORINTHIANS 1:1-16 & 3:1 - 4:21

AIM To see that Christian maturity is displayed not in division but in unity.

BIBLE STUDY Read 1:4-13
Bible Link How did division show itself in the church at Corinth?

CASE STUDY

St Saviour's has become very divided in recent months. Three years ago the Rev Graham Cartwright took over as vicar. His predecessor, Herbert Williams, had been there for twenty-two years. The church had been built during his time. His ministry was godly but rather old-fashioned. Graham has made lots of changes. The church has grown and many are in favour of what is happening, but the founder members, now in their sixties, remain loyal to their former vicar and his style of ministry. Last Autumn another group emerged shortly after some of Philip and Maureen Johnson's house group went to the New Kingdom Life convention. They feel the church is moving too slowly and needs to be more obedient to God's prophetic guidance. Each week they have been listening to tapes of convention speaker Ben Marshall. They want him to be invited to lead a Parish Renewal Weekend. Amidst all these tensions a few say: 'We are just Christians. We aren't going to get involved. We'll pray for all of you.'

ROLE PLAY the church meeting at which Maureen Johnson proposes that Ben Marshall be invited to lead a Renewal Weekend. Assign the roles of Maureen and Graham the vicar. Invite others to voice other viewpoints.

Or Develop a case study. Look at St Saviour's and ask what is happening there and why? Have you ever experienced similar problems?

Maturity Read 3:1-4
- Why are divisions a sign of a lack of spiritual maturity?

Growth
Read 3:5-15
- In what ways does real growth in the life of the church come about?

Judgement
Read 3:12-4:5
- How should God's judgement affect the way we look at our behaviour?
- How does God's judgement affect the way we look at the behaviour of others?

Boasting Read 4:6-20
- How does Paul use his own life as an example of what true discipleship means?

APPLICATION

What are the signs of growth and maturity which should mark the church's life? Are there areas in your church's life or in the attitudes you have to other Christians which should be challenged by these verses? What can you do to make sure that you are pursuing the right goals?

BEGIN HERE ALTERNATIVE When have you been drawn into taking sides in a 'personality contest' with people vying to come out on top, in work, church or family life? Share your experiences of what that felt like (perhaps in twos or threes).

ADDITIONAL QUESTIONS
Bible Link
What can we learn from 1:1-9 about
• a Christian's relationship to God?
• how God meets our needs?
• the eternal security we have as Christians?

How should Christian unity be displayed?

Maturity

• How are mature Christians described in 3:1-4? How would you recognize Christian maturity?

Growth

• What perspectives on Christian ministry does Paul give in 3:5-11? What might they mean for those involved in ministry today?
• What does it mean for Christ to be the foundation of the Church? What things can we do which will build on that foundation?

Judgement

• How can we test the quality of our Christian living?
• What difference should it make to know that we are answerable to God?

Boasting

• What are the contrasts between Paul's life and the lives of the Corinthian Christians? Which would appeal most to you? Why is Paul the one with real spiritual authority?

WORSHIP & PRAYER
Give thanks for those who have contributed to the ministry of your church over the years. (As leader you could pray a prayer which includes a time for people to mention individuals in various positions of leadership in the church both nationally and locally.) Confession of our division will almost certainly be appropriate. You could use a prayer such as *Church Family Worship* 465 or *Prayers for the People* 19.27, or write your own with the response 'Lord, forgive us; save us and help us.' Pray for those who play a part in the ministry of the church. The following list of hymns and songs might be helpful. The numbers are from the combined edition of *Mission Praise* but most will also be found in other books.

144	Fear not, rejoice and be glad	381	Jesus, stand among us
151	For I'm building a people of power	427	Lord, come and heal your church
184	God is building a house	442	Lord of the church
192	God of grace and God of glory	640	The Church's one foundation
305	I will build my church	734	We really want to thank you, Lord
376	Jesus put this song into our hearts	792	You are the Vine

Preaching Christ Crucified

1 CORINTHIANS 1:17 - 2:16

AIM To see how the message of the cross meets our need of forgiveness and new life.

INTRODUCTION

The symbol of Christianity is the cross. The heart of the Christian message is that Christ's death on that cross brings forgiveness to all those who believe in him. It is not always a welcome message. Even Christians disagree on how we should understand it. Some deride traditional ways of describing Christ's death as a sacrifice in which he took upon himself the punishment due to us because of our sins. To many with a philosophical or scholarly outlook, such views may seem too simplistic. Others object to the fact that they have to be 'saved' by someone else, rather than relying on their own goodness and efforts to live an upright life. Paul faced similar objections. To the Greeks his teaching lacked philosophical depth. To the Jews the idea of a suffering Messiah was offensive: someone crucified was under God's curse. It went against the grain of a religion based on keeping God's law. Despite such opposition Paul remained determined to preach about 'Jesus Christ and him crucified', knowing that this was God's way of reconciling humanity to himself. It was a message simple enough for ordinary people to believe and yet with real hidden depths. It was a message which met the need of human hearts for forgiveness, acceptance and the hope of eternal life. Those in whom God's Spirit was at work could see this, even if others failed to understand the great wisdom of God displayed in the cross. This message is still at the heart of Christianity.

BIBLE NOTES

1:17 Rhetorical style may impress but can create a false response, rather than life-changing faith in a crucified Christ.

1:18 Two separate eternal destinations are linked to two different responses to the message of the cross.

1:19 This is a quotation from Isaiah 29:14.

1:20-21 Wisdom and philosophy cannot deal with the problem of sin and bring people to know God, but the preached message of Jesus can.

1:22-23 The Jews demanded evidence of signs of God acting powerfully in history. To them the idea of a crucified Messiah was an impossibility. They believed the Messiah would be a man blessed by God, while a man hanged on a tree was someone cursed (see Deuteronomy 21:22-23 and Galatians 3:13). The Greeks valued philosophical wisdom. To them a message about a crucified criminal was plain foolishness.

1:24-25 Christ's death on the cross reveals God's wisdom – a wisdom which is radically different from that of human beings.

1:26 The church in Corinth (as elsewhere) was largely made up of people from lower down the social scale; though there must have been some richer people, in whose homes the church met.

1:27-29 God's choice of ordinary people demonstrated the principle that no one can stand in God's presence and boast of his or her power, riches, wisdom or social standing. We can only come to God because of Christ's death on the cross.

1:30 Our relationship with Christ is the source of a new life which brings gifts. Paul mentions the *wisdom*

of the gospel message which brings us to faith; Christ's *righteousness,* now credited to us, making it possible for us to stand before God, 'not guilty' despite all our sin; the gradual process of *sanctification* by which our lives are transformed so that we become holy; and *redemption*, which is being set free from sin. (Here redemption probably refers to the day of Christ's return when we are set free from all sin. Notice the time progression: we receive wisdom, are accounted righteous, become sanctified until the day when we are finally set free from sin.)

2:1-2 This was Paul's usual policy – not one adopted because of failure in Athens (Acts 17:22-31) as has sometimes been suggested.

2:3-5 Paul is speaking of his own feelings of inadequacy and his inability to perform as a great orator. As a result it is only because of the power of God's Spirit that they responded to his message.

2:6-8 There are levels of Christian teaching Paul could categorize as wisdom. What was once 'secret and hidden' is now something all Christians may know: the plan which God had from the beginning of time to rescue mankind through Christ. It is possible that the first three chapters of Ephesians outline the sort of wisdom the Corinthians were not ready to receive.

'Rulers of this age' may refer to the powers in the spiritual realm who seek to control events in this world, and who would not have wanted Christ crucified had they realized that his death would secure their doom. The emphasis of the passage, however, is on those who enjoy status in society, so the reference may well be to earthly authorities such as Pilate, the Jewish Sanhedrin or the Roman authorities. These rulers crucified Christ because they did not see his glory.

2:9-10a These words may be a free quotation from Isaiah 64:4, or they may come from another source now lost. Both the quotation and the following comment suggest that God's eternal purposes for those who believe are at the heart of the wisdom Paul has to teach.

2:10b-16 Just as an individual is the only one who can know and express what is in his or her own mind, so God's thoughts are known and passed on to us by the Holy Spirit. But they can only be received by a spiritual person, who is open to God's Spirit.

2:13 The Holy Spirit is seen as inspiring the preacher's words.

2:14 Some translations mention 'gifts' here, referring not so much to the charismatic gifts, as to all of God's provision.

2:15 A spiritually-aware person is a discerning person. He or she is answerable only to God (see 4:3-5).

2:16 The quotation is from Isaiah 40:13. Spiritually-minded people know the mind of Christ.

SUNDAY EXTRA

Use this week's service to help explain the significance of the death of Christ. Talk about **1. The foolishness of the cross** – why people think it is foolish. **2. The wisdom of the cross** – how it meets human need. Alternatively focus on 1:30 and how the words there show what Christ's death achieved.

For an All-age Service build up a picture of the scene at the cross on an overhead projector slide or by adding figures on a board. Talk about how various people reacted – Jesus' friends not understanding what was happening, the religious leaders and mocking soldiers. But not everyone saw it that way; talk about the differing responses of the two thieves and the centurion's conclusion, 'Surely this man was the Son of God!' (Mark 15:39)

Interview someone about what it means to them to know forgiveness because of the death of Christ. Prayers could concentrate on penitence and faith as our response to the cross, and also on the need to share that message with those around us. The hymns and songs listed in the **Worship & Prayer** section may be helpful.

Group Sheet

2

Preaching Christ Crucified

1 CORINTHIANS 1:17 - 2:16

AIM To see how the message of the cross meets our need of forgiveness and new life.

BIBLE STUDY Read 1:17-23
Bible Link Why does Christ's death on the cross present problems for people?

CASE STUDY

Dave Morgan, church warden at St Saviour's, is a down-to-earth type who left school at sixteen. He became a Christian through St Saviour's several years ago. At the time he was troubled by aspects of his past which caused him to be deeply ashamed. Learning that sins may be completely forgiven because Christ bore the penalty for them on the cross brought Dave a great sense of release. He is very frustrated at people's response when he tries to share the gospel with them. His next-door neighbours, Simon and Helen Middleton, are university graduates. Simon dismisses any talk of Christ dying for us as unethical: 'How can someone else take your place. You must take the consequences of your own sin. Besides, how could a loving God punish his own son?' Helen has been influenced by current thinking and argues that Christianity is guilt-driven, obsessed with sin: 'We don't need to be reconciled to God, we just need to recognize the divine that is within each of us.' Even Dave's friend Tony who goes to a neighbouring church occasionally argues that all God wants of us is to live a decent life. The cross is just an example of how far we must go in loving.

ROLE PLAY the discussion between Dave, Simon, Helen and Tony over coffee after a meal at Dave's house or the discussion at his housegroup when Dave talks about how difficult it is to share his faith.

Or discuss the different understandings of Christ's death which are represented in the case study. How do your non-Christian friends think about Christ's death?

Wisdom Read 1:24-25
● How does the cross show God's wisdom? What problems does it address?

No Boasting Read 1:26-31
● Does the cross challenge human boasting? If so, why does it matter?

New Life Read 1:30
● 'Wisdom', 'righteousness', 'holiness', 'redemption': what do these words mean here? (You may need some reference books to help!) How does the fact that Jesus actually *is* all of these things make a difference in our lives?

Preaching Christ
Read 2:1-16
● What role does the Holy Spirit play in helping people believe? How do these verses encourage us to share our faith with others despite our own feelings of inadequacy?

APPLICATION

What are the significant achievements of Christ's death on the cross? How might these insights help you as you talk to others about Christ?

BEGIN HERE ALTERNATIVE When have you been made to feel that the Christian message is foolish? What did people say that made you feel that?

ADDITIONAL QUESTIONS
Bible Link
Why is God opposed to the clever and the wise (1:18-21)? Is academic learning a waste of time, or is Paul saying something else here?

Wisdom

- What makes the gospel message powerful? How did it make an impact on your life?

No Boasting

- Is Paul right to say that the gospel has a special appeal to people who are less well-off? Is there evidence of this in today's world?
- Why do intellectuals and the affluent often find it hard to believe?

New Life

- How does 1:30 speak of the fact that there are both 'now' and 'not yet' elements to our salvation? How does the assurance that we are accounted righteous before God encourage us now and as we look to the future?

Preaching Christ

- Why do you think Paul did not find it easy to preach about Christ (2:1-5)? Why do we find it hard?
- Which aspects of Christian faith might we be tempted to emphasise, rather than preaching first about Christ's crucifixion? Why might this be? How can we share Paul's determination to preach about a crucified Christ?
- What is the 'hidden' or 'secret' wisdom of God which Paul mentions in 2:6-7?
- How does Paul describe the 'spiritual' and the 'unspiritual' person in 2:8-16? What are the differences between them?

WORSHIP & PRAYER
Much of this week's study should promote thankfulness for the cross. Get the group to pray short prayers of thanks for what Christ's death means to them, perhaps completing the sentence 'Thank you that because Christ died ...'. Use a hymn such as 'When I survey the wondrous cross' (*Mission Praise* 745) or 'O sacred head, once wounded' (*Mission Praise* 520) as a meditation. Pray for those whom you know who think the message of Christ's death foolish. Songs chosen from the list below will also help the group respond to the message about the cross.

21	All the riches of his grace	458	Man of Sorrows
26	All you that pass by	476	My Lord, what love is this
31	Amazing grace	632	Thank you for the cross
222	He was pierced	738	We sing the praise
346	It is a thing most wonderful	745	Were you there
351	It's your blood that cleanses me	755	When I survey the wondrous cross

Upright Behaviour

1 CORINTHIANS 5:1 - 6:19

AIM To discover the standards of behaviour expected among Christians.

INTRODUCTION

Christian moral standards tend to lag a few steps behind those of society. Sadly, in the end the church often conforms to what the world is doing. This passage challenges us about such a process, showing that Christian morality gives us different standards from those around us. This flows from the inward transformation of our characters brought about by Christ. We have a responsibility to present the consistent witness of holy lives. While we may regret the glee the press shows over the latest 'naughty vicar' scandal, there is some justification for their horror (often mock!) when Christians fall from traditional standards of morality. The church must be seen to live its message. Of course Christians will fail, but this passage suggests that failure is not something to be condoned or accepted with a shrug. Paul sets a standard of church discipline which is stricter than anything many Christians today find acceptable or practicable. Even if we are unable to follow such a practice of discipline fully, we cannot ignore sinful behaviour and have to find some way of dealing with it in the life of the church. These are the difficult issues Christians have to face in a society where moral standards are rapidly changing.

BIBLE NOTES

5:1 Corinth was renowned for its immorality. Its lax standards were bound to affect Christians, but even pagans would not approve of someone committing adultery with his step-mother.

5:2-5 Paul pronounces sentence of excommunication (exclusion from fellowship) on the man in question. Though far away, Paul is present in spirit at the solemn meeting at which the ban should be pronounced.

5:5 The world beyond the Church is dominated by Satan, the 'god of this world' (2 Corinthians 4:4). The destruction of 'the flesh' or 'sinful nature' may mean that the man will be brought to his senses and will decide to put to death his physical desires. Or Paul may envisage sickness as the consequence (see 1 Corinthians 12:7), or even death (as with Ananias and Sapphira in Acts 5:1-11). But ultimately on the day of judgement this person will be saved because those who belong to Christ are his for ever.

5:6-8 Yeast (leaven) has a very pervasive effect and is often used as a picture of the spread of evil. All yeast has to be removed from a Jewish home before Passover and a fresh start made afterwards with a new lump of unleavened dough. So Christians need to be free of sin ('unleavened') – which in fact is what they are, a holy people, who have no business falling into sin. Indeed Christ their Passover sacrifice has already been offered as he died upon the cross, so that they had better hurry to get rid of any left-over 'yeast' by amending their lives at once – it should have been got rid of already!

5:9-11 Paul refers to an earlier letter to the Corinthians; some had assumed he was urging total separation from non-Christians. Paul stresses that he was referring to immoral Christians – everyday life is bound to involve contact with immoral people.

5:12-13 The judgement of non-Christians is in God's hands, but Christians are responsible for discipline within the church. Verse 13 echoes Deuteronomy 17:7 and 22:24.

6:1-8 Greeks were very quick to take their grievances to court and so were the Corinthian Christians! Jews normally dealt with disputes within their own community. Paul sees this as preferable to washing dirty linen in public.

6:2 This is based on passages such as Daniel 7:22, where the saints share in judgement, and Jesus' words about the disciples sharing in judgement (Matthew 19:28 and Luke 22:28-30).

6:3 Christians will even judge angels, the highest class of created beings.

6:7 Christ taught us to turn the other cheek and to give up cloak as well as coat (Matthew 5:39-40). Therefore going to court is to desert Christian principles.

6:9-10 Paul speaks of the 'wicked' ('unrighteous') as a description of all sinful people. He defines several categories of sinners. The list includes two Greek words (for which one word is used in some translations) which suggest the active and passive roles in homosexual activity.

6:11 Some Corinthian Christians had been converted from an obviously sinful lifestyle. They had been 'washed', a reference to the inward significance of baptism; 'sanctified', not a reference here to the process of sanctification but to becoming one of God's holy ('sanctified') people; and 'justified', declared to be just before God because of their faith in Christ. They must now live this out.

6:12 'All things are lawful' seems to have been a watch-word in Corinth. It may have derived from Paul's teaching that Christians are not bound to keep the whole Jewish law in order to be saved, but are free, for example, to eat what they like. They may also have been influenced by the philosophy known as 'Gnosticism', which claimed that the spirit is of more value than the body – so it does not matter what we do with our bodies from which death will one day release us. Paul affirms Christian freedom from legalism, but adds the qualification that not all things are helpful; some enslave us.

6:13 Food may be meant for the stomach, but the body is not necessarily meant for sex. It is to be used for the Lord.

6:14 In Christian thinking bodies do matter. One day they will be raised to life.

6:15-17 There is such a close identification between Christ and the believer that Paul says they are members of Christ's body. It is therefore unthinkable to have sex with a prostitute because sex creates a unity between two people (Genesis 2:24).

6:18-20 Sexual sin is a misuse of the body 'indwelt' by Christ through the Holy Spirit, and therefore his temple. In any case we are not free to do as we please: we are God's slaves, bought by him at the price of the blood of Christ (see Acts 20:28; 1 Peter 1:18-19). We must therefore glorify God by what we do with our bodies.

SUNDAY EXTRA

In this week's services talk about the Passover custom of cleaning out the yeast from the home and the need for us to clean out all the wrong things in our lives when we have experienced the deliverance brought about by Christ, our Passover lamb (5:7). In a sermon for adults go on to talk about **1. Cleaning out the old** (5:7) **2. Celebrating with the new** (5:8). In All-age Worship go on to compile together a list those things which should be **OUT** for Christians and those things which should be **IN**.

Testimony of how Christ changes lives might help – either given by a member of the congregation or taken from a book. Pray about morality and justice in the lives of individuals, church and nation. Some of the hymns and songs listed in the **Worship & Prayer** section may be helpful.

Group Sheet

3

Upright Behaviour

1 CORINTHIANS 5:1 - 6:19

AIM To discover the standards of behaviour expected among Christians.

CASE STUDY

St Saviour's is in a turmoil over two affairs which threaten to reach the newspapers. Alan Robinson, the organist, appears to have been having an affair with Rachel, a fourteen-year-old choir girl. His wife has just left him and he and Rachel have often been seen together. Rachel's parents are very upset and have been to see Graham Cartwright, the vicar. They suspect Alan and Rachel have been sleeping together. Graham challenged Alan but was told, 'It's nobody else's business but our own. What can be wrong if we love each other? Besides Christians need to realize times have changed.' Some in the church would agree, feeling rules and regulations do not matter. Others feel reluctant to interfere in other people's lives. A few think there is probably nothing to worry about.

Meanwhile another blow has fallen. Two members of the church are involved in a court case. Philip Henry, a plumber, has often done jobs for church warden David Freeman, owner of a small building company. Philip is taking David to court over non-payment for a recent piece of work. Many in the church feel David has traded on their common church involvement as an excuse for delaying payment. Others feel Philip should be more sympathetic to David and should wait until trade starts looking up. A reporter has been calling members to ask what is going on at St Saviour's.

ROLE PLAY the discussion between Graham Cartwright, his Bishop and Diocesan Press Officer Susan Morrison, whom Graham has called in to advise him on how to handle both situations.

Or discuss why some Christians might condone or at least ignore the behaviour of Alan Robinson and Philip Henry. How are readers of the newspapers likely to react? Why? What issues are at stake here?

BIBLE STUDY
Read 5:1 and 6:1-6

Bible Link What was causing Paul concern in the behaviour of some Christians in Corinth?

Discipline Read 5:1-13
- Why is Paul arguing for the exercise of discipline in church life? How can we demonstrate both discipline and forgiveness?

Grievances Read 6:1-8
- Why should we sort out grievances within the church? How can we go about this?

Changed Lives Read 6:9-11
- What do these verses show about the way God can change people? How does it come about?

Immorality Read 6:12-20
- What reasons does Paul give to show that immorality is not an appropriate exercise of Christian 'freedom'?

APPLICATION
How can the church present an image which is both attractive and consistent with high moral standards? In what ways should we be different from those around us?

BEGIN HERE ALTERNATIVE What sort of failures on the part of Christians are pounced upon by the media or your non-Christian friends and neighbours?

ADDITIONAL QUESTIONS
Bible Link
Why does Paul feel the behaviour mentioned here is unacceptable?

Discipline

- Why might Christians condone or ignore immoral behaviour? What ought to be our reaction to sin in our lives and the lives of other Christians?
- What does Paul hope the exercise of discipline will achieve?
- Why may we associate with immoral non-Christians when we should not associate with immoral Christians?

Grievances

- What sort of people in the church could we turn to for help when grievances arise between us?

Changed Lives

- Does the church include those whose former life-styles Paul describes in 6:9-10? How can we reach out to people whose way of life conflicts with Christian standards, while still maintaining those standards ourselves?
- Do you know any stories which show the transforming power Paul speaks of in 6:11? They may be from your own experience, or they may be ones you have read or heard about.

Immorality

- What does it mean for a Christian to be 'free from the law'? What is Christian 'freedom' really about?
- How do Paul's words challenge the casual attitude to sex prevalent in today's society?
- How does the fact that we belong to God (6:20) change our perspective on the way we live?

WORSHIP & PRAYER
Once again confession is probably an appropriate response to this week's theme. Why not use a form of confession familiar to your group? (*Mission Praise* 28 is the confession from the *Alternative Service Book*.) You could also sing the Caribbean Lord's Prayer (*Mission Praise* 552) with pauses between the verses for silent or open prayer. Pray that clergy and laity in positions of leadership in the church will be kept free from sin. Pray also that Christians will be able to stand firm for biblical moral standards.

3	Abba Father	192	God of grace and God of glory
28	Almighty God, our heavenly Father	254	I am a new creation
82	Cleanse me from my sin	449	Love divine, all loves excelling
108	Create in me a clean heart	494	O for a closer walk with God
110	Darkness like a shroud	587	Search me, O God
186	God is in his temple	743	We'll walk the land

Faithful for Life

1 CORINTHIANS 7

AIM To see the value of singleness and of faithful marriage relationships.

INTRODUCTION

'Why get married?' is a question often raised these days. That marriage is an outdated, irrelevant, discredited institution seems to be an increasingly popular viewpoint. Most young couples live together, at least at first, rather than get married. Divorce is the common way marriages end. The Corinthian church also asked, 'Why get married?', but from a different perspective. In contrast to the group addressed at the end of Chapter 6 with their free attitude to sex, there were those in the church who felt sex was wrong and best avoided. A relationship which did not include sex might be acceptable, but obviously it was not easy to resist temptation. 'Is it OK to get married?' they asked. 'Is it OK to get divorced?' asked others. 'And what about non-Christian partners?' pondered yet another group. Paul tackles these questions and provides some insights on marriage which may help us as we face today's questions in this area. Paul accepts that the sexual drive cannot always be resisted, but stresses that the right context for sex is marriage. Marriage is for life, though there seems to be some leeway about divorce when a non-Christian partner is involved. Singleness is to be highly valued too. This whole area is one in which Christians are called to be different from those around them.

BIBLE NOTES

7:1-2 Paul may well be quoting the Corinthians when he says, 'It is well for a man not to touch a woman' ('not to marry' in some translations). Such asceticism may have been a reaction of some to the 'liberal' attitudes of others. Paul suggests that while chastity is valuable, most of us will find marriage inevitable because we cannot deny our sexual desires!

7:3-4 Husbands and wives have obligations to each other. Sexual relations are a key part of married life.

7:5-6 Forgoing sex even to give time to extended prayer is allowed only as a concession, and then for a very limited period.

7:7 Marriage and celibacy are described as 'charismata', gifts from God. Neither is more holy. Some, like Paul, have the gift for celibacy, others for marriage.

7:8 Paul values singleness. He was single, though we don't know whether this was as a bachelor or a widower.

7:9 In contrast to some Christian traditions, Paul sees no special merit in suppressing sexual desire. Marriage is, however, seen as the only context in which a sexual relationship can take place.

7:10-11 Paul speaks here of situations where both partners are Christians and he refers to Christ's teaching (Mark 10:2-12). In these circumstances remarriage after separation is not seen as an option.

7:12-13 While a marriage with a non-Christian is on a different footing, it should not be broken if the non-Christian partner is happy with it.

7:14 Paul seems to be working on the Old Testament principle that the blessings of God's covenant relationship extend beyond an individual to the family. Children were certainly included within that covenant relationship and, by extension, an unbelieving partner is here included as well.

7:15 When the non-Christian partner chooses divorce, the Christian is not bound to that marriage and may possibly be free to remarry. The woman's position here is probably being seen as one of widowhood. There may be a similar principle underlying the exception Jesus makes in allowing divorce on the grounds of adultery in Matthew 5:32 and 19:9. In Old Testament law the penalty for adultery was death. The surviving partner was therefore free to marry again. So in days when the adulterous partner is not put to death the other partner is still free to marry after divorce.

7:16 A mixed marriage in this situation may bring the non-Christian partner to faith.

7:17 Believers should be content to remain in the position they were in when they came to faith – married or unmarried, slave or free, as verses 18-24 (not included in this study) demonstrate.

7:25 Unlike the topic of divorce, there is no direct teaching from Christ on this subject.

7:26-31 Paul mentions impending distress. This may be the expectation of a time of tribulation preceding the return of Christ, or it may be a time of persecution. Such troubles may affect how we respond in many situations, possibly making marriage inadvisable. However it can never be regarded as sinful to marry.

7:32-35 Single people have a greater freedom in some respects to serve God.

7:36-38 Paul is addressing either fathers with unmarried daughters or, more probably, those who are engaged but reluctant to go ahead with the marriage because of the anti-sex teaching in the church at Corinth. To withhold marriage from a girl of marriageable age would be considered scandalous. All sorts of pressures may dictate marriage as the right option – in other situations refraining from marriage may be better.

7:39-40 Widows are free to marry but only 'in the Lord', that is to someone else who is a Christian.

SUNDAY EXTRA

We are often accused of not talking about Christian attitudes to sex. This week's passage gives us the opportunity to do so and to talk about **1. Sex for the married 2. Sex for the single** or to tackle issues concerning marriage and divorce.

For Family Worship use an overhead projector slide with flaps to add or remove pictures of faces (or use faces on a board) to talk about our 'ideal' for the Christian family – with a Christian mum and dad and Christian children. Go on to explain that many families are not in that position and this passage shows that it is OK when one partner becomes a Christian after marriage, or a marriage breaks up or a partner dies, and how it is good to be single too. Aim to show that God knows and cares about us in every situation.

As an additional activity this week you might like to ask everyone to talk in small groups about the best and the worst things about being in a family. Prayer about marriage and family life will obviously be appropriate. The songs and hymns from *Mission Praise* listed under **Worship & Prayer** may be useful.

Faithful for Life

1 CORINTHIANS 7

AIM To see the value of singleness and of faithful marriage relationships.

CASE STUDY

Andy Grey and Susan Thompson are two of the most committed Christian young people at St Saviour's. They have been going out for several years and not long ago announced their engagement. Before they get married, however, Andy is keen to fulfil a long-held ambition to spend several years as an overseas aid worker. Susan has always supported him in this plan. But recently they have been wondering if they are right to put off marriage: whenever they spend time together, they are finding it harder and harder not to 'go too far'. They decide to join the queue of other couples at the vicar's weekly 'surgery' hour. Also there is an older couple: Wendy Harper and Jack Rossiter. Wendy is a widow and a long-standing member of St Saviour's. Jack started coming three years ago when he became a Christian following a marriage break-up. After attempts at reconciliation with his wife had failed, he met and fell in love with Wendy. Now they are wondering whether it is possible for them to get married in church.

ROLE PLAY the conversations between Andy and Susan and between Wendy and Jack which led to them going to see the vicar or else the conversation between the two couples as they wait to meet the vicar.

Or discuss the marriage-related issues which set Christians apart from non-Christians. Do Christians eventually adapt their standards to those of society, or are there things for which we must continue to stand firm?

BIBLE STUDY

Read 7:8-9 and 39-40

Bible Link What are the basic guidelines Paul gives here about marriage among Christians? How do they cause problems in today's climate of thinking?

Sex Read 7:1-9 and 36-38
- How does sex have its right place within marriage? Is marriage just an outlet for our sexual urges?

Separation Read 7:10-11
- What situations can you envisage in which separation is the only answer?

Salvation Read 7:12-17
- Why should a Christian remain with a non-Christian partner? What pressures are there in such situations? Why does Paul seem to give some limited scope for remarriage after divorce in verse 15 as Jesus does in Matthew 19:9?

Singleness Read 7:25-35
- What are the benefits of being single? Do we undervalue singleness?

APPLICATION

How can Paul's guidelines help us address questions about marriage in the life of the church today? What is the underlying motivation behind all Paul's advice?

 BEGIN HERE ALTERNATIVE You sometimes hear sayings such as, 'Marriage is an institution – but who wants to live in an institution?' or 'Christianity is anti-sex!' How do such remarks reflect the way people today think?

 ADDITIONAL QUESTIONS
Bible Link
Is Paul anti-marriage and anti-sex, as some people argue? How does Ephesians 5:21-33 modify our picture of Paul's understanding of marriage?

Is it realistic to expect Christians to marry only Christians? Why does Paul give this as a norm?

Sex

- What role does sex play in a Christian marriage? Is it just a duty?
- In what ways are marriage *and* singleness gifts from God (7:7)?

Separation

- What problems face people after bereavement or separation from a living partner? What sort of support might be needed for those in this position?

Salvation

- What things create tensions in a marriage between a Christian and a non-Christian? How can the Christian partner in such a marriage be an effective witness for Christ?

Singleness

- What situations can you envisage where Paul's advice (7:25-31) would make good sense?
- Do you know people who have been able to serve the Lord better because they are single? Does marriage detract from our service to God?

 WORSHIP & PRAYER
Many feel that in society today the institution of marriage is under attack. Spend some time praying about this and for the church's witness in this area. To set the scene, you could read Ephesians 5:21-33 as a meditation as it shows how marriage witnesses to Christ's love for his Church. Pray for single people, younger and older, and for those divorced and bereaved too.

60	Blest be the tie that binds	335	In my life Lord, be glorified
111	Dear Lord and Father of mankind	382	Jesus take me as I am
133	Father, I place into your hands	407	Let me have my way among you
146	Fill thou my life	517	O perfect Love
263	I am weak but thou art strong	541	One shall tell another
304	I want to worship the Lord	624	Take my life, and let it be

5 Limited Freedom

1 CORINTHIANS 8:1 - 11:1

AIM To learn consideration for the needs and thinking of other people.

INTRODUCTION

Is it right to eat meat which has been offered to idols? It's not a common dilemma in today's Western world! For the Corinthians, however, the question caused real problems. Many social events were held in local temples. Much of the meat on sale in the butchers' shops was excess meat from sacrifices, 'sold on' by the temple authorities. So-called strong Christians argued that as idols were nothing, there was no problem in eating such meat. Others (often those newer to the faith) still felt something of the power and attraction of idolatrous worship and were more sensitive about not being seen to compromise an exclusive loyalty to Christ. They were uneasy in their consciences, not 'strong-minded' or defiant enough to eat such meat and so were considered to be 'weaker' brothers and sisters. Paul tackles this theme again in Romans 14:1-15:7. As well as the meat problem, he also discusses divisions over drinking wine and observing a liturgical calendar of feast days and fast days.

Many Christians have turned to this passage when they have urged fellow believers to abstain from alcohol in case their example causes others to fall. (They have often added other 'worldly' temptations to the list of things to be avoided.) Is such an argument still relevant? Much current thinking encourages us to discover new freedom and our real 'personhood' in Christ, to be distinct individuals who express ourselves and do what we feel is right. Paul encourages us to see that we cannot always stand on our personal rights. How do we deal with 'weak' Christians who have strong opinions about things? Do we ignore or even look down on them for their old-fashioned attitudes? Paul argues here that we must consider the thoughts of others. We must be wary too – those who take a superior attitude are the most likely to fall. Our prime concern must be the good of others, not our own freedom.

BIBLE NOTES

8:1-3 Christians may possess the special insight of 'knowledge', but it is love, not knowledge, which is truly constructive.

8:4-13 Like some of the Corinthians, Paul agrees that as there is only one God, idols are nothing. Not all have this firm understanding, however. Formerly accustomed to idol-worship, they cannot now in good conscience eat food offered to an idol. People matter more than food and to cause a fellow-believer to stumble is to sin against Christ, who treats harm done to his people as harm done to him.

8:10 Feasts were held in temples, the meat having been dedicated to the temple gods. Strong Christians, knowing these gods did not exist, could take a superior attitude and join in, despising those who thought the idols were real. Such an example might cause Christians who still attributed some power to the temple deities to eat and feel guilty, or even to be drawn away from Christ.

9:1-6 Apostles and their wives had the right to be supported by their fellow Christians but Paul did not claim that right. Some obviously disputed his claim to be an apostle, but the fact that he had seen the risen Christ and the evidence of his successful ministry, particularly in Corinth, showed God had given him the responsibility of apostleship. Cephas is the apostle Peter.

9:7-14 Paul uses the examples of the soldier, farmer and shepherd to defend the right of Christian ministers to be supported. He also cites the Jewish Law which allowed a working animal a share of what it helped to

produce: he draws a parallel with the situation which allowed Christian workers to be fed while doing their work. A further example was the Law's provision for the priests. Finally he cites Christ's own command, probably a reference to Luke 10:7, 'the labourer deserves his wages'.

9:15-18 Having established his rights Paul disowns them. He preached because of an inner compulsion and a commission entrusted to him. Doing so without payment has brought its own reward.

9:19-23 Paul wanted to share the gospel with a whole variety of people and was willing to live and eat as they did in order to get alongside them.

9:24-27 The Isthmian games were held in the area every two years and demanded high athletic standards. The prize was a wreath made of pine.

10:1-5 Paul uses the Old Testament to show that people who have been blessed spiritually can still fail. As baptism brings us under the leadership of Christ and sets us free to live a new life, so the Israelites followed Moses and had their equivalent of baptism as they left behind the old life in Egypt when they were guided by the cloud (see Exodus 13:21-22) and passed through the sea (Exodus 14). There were equivalents of Holy Communion too. They were given food and drink by God who provided both manna and quail (Exodus 16) and water out of the rock (Exodus 17:1-7 and Numbers 20:8-11). From these references Jewish tradition developed the idea that the same rock followed the Israelites wherever they went. Paul is not necessarily endorsing this tradition but he does identify Christ as the one who was with them, meeting their needs, material and spiritual.

10:6-8 These verses point out the dangers of idol worship, something very pertinent to the situation in Corinth. The references are to the worship of the golden calf (Exodus 32:6) and to the occasion when the Israelites joined in the idolatrous worship of the Midianites (Numbers 25:1-9).

10:9-10 Here to 'put God to the test' is a matter of cynically seeing how far you can go before God acts on his word and punishes: Paul refers in verse 9 to Numbers 21:5-9. There are many references to God's response to those who 'murmur' against him (verse 10), such as Numbers 11:1-3, 14:1-35, 16:1-35 and 41-50.

10:11-13 The Old Testament examples are a warning of the dangers into which God's people so easily fall, but which can be avoided with his help.

10:14-22 Paul points out the sacredness of sharing in the Lord's Supper, which unites believers in fellowship with Christ and with one another. Such sharing is incompatible with eating in a pagan temple. While there may be no other gods, there are demonic forces behind idolatrous worship and one must not have fellowship with demons.

10:23-11:1 Having prohibited joining in meals in temples, Paul gives commonsense guidelines about domestic meals, allowing any meat to be bought and eaten at home unless it is pointed out that it has been offered to an idol. Someone may do that because of their own conscience or as a test of a Christian's commitment to Christ. In such cases Christians should put the peace of a more sensitive conscience before the freedom of their own more robust convictions.

SUNDAY EXTRA

Focus on 10:1-13 in this week's worship. For an adult sermon talk about human nature never changing and point out that, despite the grace given by God, there are temptations to compromise and follow the standards of our surrounding society. The passage shows that to be true: **1. In Old Testament times 2. In Corinth 3. Today.** Alternatively follow the theme of the whole section and talk about **Rights and Responsibilities**.

For All-age Worship talk about the temptations the Israelites faced. List temptations we face and then write across it 'Say no – with God's help' and talk about the teaching given in 10:13.

Pray for those who have failed to resist temptation, such as those in prison, addicted to drugs – and us! Choose hymns and songs from the list in the **Worship & Prayer** section.

5

Group Sheet

Limited Freedom

1 CORINTHIANS 8:1 - 11:1

AIM To learn consideration for the needs and thinking of other people.

CASE STUDY
Graham Cartwright, vicar of St Saviour's, is chairing a rather sticky meeting of the support group for Tim Simpson, the church's youth leader. Tim was appointed because he seemed to have 'street cred' with the young people and an enthusiastic desire to relate Christianity to the modern culture familiar to them. He has been keen to explore the freedom Christ gives us to be ourselves: to some of the parents his dress and behaviour seem a little too unconventional. Tim has been taking members of the group to local concerts. Some have gone with him to parties held by some of his non-Christian friends. Dave Morgan, the church warden, has recently had several phone calls from worried parents. Tonight he has passed them on to the support group. Some of the young people have started smoking and drinking, using the claim that 'Tim's friends do' as justification. One or two report having been offered drugs at concerts and parties. Clare Eastwood, one of the mothers on the support group, is very unhappy and says that some of the parents are thinking of moving to the Baptist Church where they take a stricter line on such behaviour. Debbie Walker springs to Tim's defence: 'My kids think he's wonderful. The teaching sessions they have had about using our creative gifts and developing an authentically Christian lifestyle have been really exciting. He has used the experiences the youngsters have had to open up good discussions about the use of recreational drugs and about Christian standards.'

ROLE PLAY the support meeting and develop the expression of concern about Tim's leadership.

Or identify and discuss the issues about Christian freedom and responsibility demonstrated by Tim's leadership of the youth group? Why are people divided? Are there other issues which cause division among Christians?

BIBLE STUDY Read 8:1-8
Bible Link What was the issue concerning freedom and conscience which divided the church in Corinth?

Concern Read 8:9-13
- How should those who are 'strong' behave to those with more tender consciences?

Consideration
Read 9:1-26
- How does Paul's example of taking no payment for his ministry illustrate the consideration we should have for others?

Temptation Read 10:1-22
- What is the warning Paul gives to the strong here? Can you give examples from your own experience of spiritual pride going before a fall?

Freedom Read 10:23 - 11:1
- In what ways are Christians free to decide for themselves how they will act and in what ways should that freedom be limited?

APPLICATION
How do the principles in this passage help us handle those issues of conscience and behaviour over which Christians have valid grounds for disagreement? What must be our overriding concern?

BEGIN HERE ALTERNATIVE

Over the years what has been on the list of things 'good Christians shouldn't do'? Have our taboos changed over the years and if so, why?

ADDITIONAL QUESTIONS

Bible Link Why is an emphasis on knowledge not always helpful?

What do we learn from these verses about God and about idols?

Concern

- What things might we do unintentionally which could lead someone else into spiritual difficulties?

Consideration

- What does Paul teach about how those in Christian ministry can normally expect support? What is Paul's concern in not receiving such support?
- How does he demonstrate his desire to share the gospel? Does this give us any guidelines for how we go about our evangelism?

Temptation

- How does Paul's use of the Old Testament demonstrate how the Bible has relevance and can help shape our lives?
- How do we learn to escape temptation?
- How can we ensure that our behaviour is consistent with our worship?

Freedom

- Is Paul setting a double standard for public and private behaviour in his guidelines in these verses? If you disagree, say why.

WORSHIP & PRAYER

Part of the study focused on temptation. Lead a prayer which mentions various temptations we face (perhaps drawing on aspects of your discussion). Begin each section of the prayer 'When we are tempted to...' and use as a response after each section, 'Lead us not into temptation: But deliver us from evil'. Pray for greater understanding among Christians. Express your own acceptance of each other by exchanging the 'Peace' with words such as 'The Peace of the Lord be with you'. There are suitable songs listed below.

1	A new commandment I give unto you	410	Let the beauty of Jesus
7	All creatures of our God and King	501	O Jesus, I have promised
8	All earth was dark	553	Peace, I give to you
329	In Christ there is no East or West	637	Thanks be to God
376	Jesus put this song into our hearts	678	There's a quiet understanding
381	Jesus, stand among us	734	We really want to thank you

5

6

Orderly Worship

1 CORINTHIANS 11:2-33 & 14:20-40

AIM To value the needs of the whole church, and to appreciate the need for order in our worship.

INTRODUCTION

Disagreements over worship are all too common. Who can contribute? What is the place of women in the leadership of worship? How free or how ordered should it be? Is there room for the use of spiritual gifts such as tongues and prophecy? Such problems are not new. In Corinth where the church met in homes there was scope for freedom and for everyone to contribute but this freedom led to problems. Paul addresses questions over the way in which women took part, the division between rich and poor at the Lord's Supper and the abuse of the gifts of tongues and prophecy. He argues for unity and for order so that worship is positively upbuilding. These are principles we should still heed.

BIBLE NOTES

11:2 The Corinthians claim to have been keeping the traditions of belief and practice passed on to them by Paul. He praises them for that. The following verses suggest that they had asked whether, as a sign of women's freedom and equality in Christ, they could abandon the custom that women who prayed or prophesied should have their heads covered. They may have already been doing so.

11:3-16 These verses are not easy to follow. It helps if we understand the normal practice of those times. Respectable women had long hair which was covered by a veil when they were in public. Or, as some writers suggest, their hair may have been put up but not covered. Either way it was normally only a husband who saw a woman with her hair down. It was only prostitutes or convicted adulteresses who had short hair (see 11:5 and 6). To let your hair down in public was a shameful thing.

Much of this section is based on a theological argument about our role in creation. The original Greek of 11:3 refers to God as the 'head' of Christ, Christ as the 'head' of man, and man as the 'head' of woman. Traditionally this has been taken to refer to a chain of superiority (as suggested in the *Good News Bible* translation). To use 'head' in this sense is, however, rare in Greek writing and would also make Christ inferior to God the Father. It is probably more helpful to interpret head as 'the source from which something comes'. Thus Christ 'proceeds' from the Father, as the Nicene Creed says. Christ, as the agent in creation, created man. Woman was created out of man to be his companion (Genesis 2:21-23). Verses 11 and 12 speak of the interdependence and equality of men and women and this helps us make better sense of verse 3 where the relationship between man and woman can be seen to parallel the interdependence and equality of God the Father and Christ.

Each in his place then reflects the glory of the other. Colossians 1:15-20 speaks of Christ as the image of God, here Paul speaks of man as the image and glory of God, a glory he reflects by worshipping with unveiled face (see 2 Corinthians 3:12-18). However the beauty of a woman with her hair down is something only to be shared with her husband – it is his glory (11:7). When she speaks in church with her head covered she does so with the authority that comes from playing her own proper role as a woman – she does not have to uncover her hair to be like a man in order to exercise her authority to speak (11:10). The reference to angels in 11:10 is to the fact that we worship 'with angels and archangels and with all the host of heaven' and so we should do so in a way which reflects God's ordering of things. Paul backs up his argument with an appeal to the normal pattern of men having short hair and women long hair (11:13-15) and a final definitive statement that this is how all churches do things (11:16).

11:17-19 Divisions in the church are not to be commended, even if they sometimes lead to a clarification of what is right and what is wrong.

11:20-22 The Lord's Supper was celebrated as part of a fellowship meal (or *agape*). Like the Last Supper it was a proper meal. The rich could come early to the meal and brought most of the food. Slaves and workers could only come when work was done, by which time all the food had gone and the rich were getting drunk! This abuse led to the later separation of the Holy Communion from the communal meal – a development of Paul's suggestions in 11:22 and 33-34.

11:23-26 These verses give the earliest written account of the Last Supper and Christ's instruction to continue observing it in remembrance of him. Christ's words that it is 'for you' speak of his death as a sacrifice. He refers to the establishing of the new covenant promised in Jeremiah 31:31-34. Our repetition of it acts, as did the Passover, as a 'remembrance', not just a remembering but a positive rejoicing in and entering into what Christ has done for us. It is a proclamation (11:26), powerfully preaching Christ's death.

11:27-34 Sickness and even death (seen as just a falling asleep for Christians) are the judgement upon those who come lightly to the Lord's Supper. We must recognize 'the body of the Lord' (11:29) in the sense of recognizing one another as the body of Christ (see 10:16-17). The Lord's Supper is a sign of our unity, so we must examine ourselves to see if we are 'in love and charity with our neighbour'.

14:20 Concentrating on the gifts of tongues is a sign of immaturity.

14:21-25 Isaiah 28:11-12, quoted here, refers to the foreign speech of the Assyrian invaders as a sign of judgement on an unbelieving people, confirming them in their disobedience. In the same way unbelievers will be confirmed in their unbelief as they conclude Christians are mad when they hear them speaking in tongues. Prophecy, however, which is intended in the first place to strengthen believers is also capable of speaking directly to the heart of non-Christians, bringing them to faith.

14:26-28 Worship in the early church was in the smaller setting of the home, and so allowed everyone to contribute. However everyone speaking in tongues at once was not helpful. It should be done one at a time by only two or three people, with someone exercising the gift of interpretation of tongues. If no one has that gift then tongues should only be used in personal prayer.

14:29-33a Prophecy too can be overdone – only two or three should speak. Prophets are in control of what they do and say. It cannot be argued that they 'have to pass on the message', thus leading to disorder. Others must judge the value of what is said.

14:33b-35 Paul in 11:5 allows women to pray and prophesy, so the order about silence is not absolute. The reference is possibly to women (who were often less well-educated) chatting because they did not understand or else asking too many questions. Home is the right place for such discussion.

14:36-40 Paul appeals to the common tradition of the churches, to his God-given authority to speak as an apostle and to the need for order.

SUNDAY EXTRA
Talk this week about worship and the principles shaping it. **1. Openness to God** (14:39) **2. Openness to others** (14:26) **3. Order** (14:33 and 40).

If you prefer focus on the Service of Holy Communion which speaks of **1. Forgiveness** (11:23-25) **2. Fellowship** (11:17-22, 33-34 and 10:16-17) **3. The Future** (11:26).

In an All-age service you might like to teach about worship and Holy Communion by explaining each section of the Holy Communion service as you work your way through it.

You could ask everyone to share in small groups why they come to church or one thing they enjoy about worship. In the prayers give thanks for the privilege of worship, pray for those who lead and take part in worship. Use some of the songs and hymns from the list in the **Worship & Prayer** section.

6

Group Sheet

Orderly Worship

1 CORINTHIANS 11:2-33 & 14:20-40

AIM To value the needs of the whole church, and to appreciate the need for order in our worship.

Why do the traditionalist group feel unhappy? Do they have some justification for their unease?

CASE STUDY

Things are not improving for Graham Cartwright, vicar of St Saviour's. The Bishop has given him the good news that the parish is to have the much-needed help of a curate, a recently-ordained woman priest. Graham is quite happy about that, as are most of the congregation but he suspects that the more traditional members of the church (the ones loyal to Herbert Williams, his predecessor) will be uneasy. To head off trouble he has invited a few of them to the vicarage for a chat. They have accepted the invitation very readily because they have been looking for a chance to put the vicar straight about the things that have been happening in the church's worship lately. The Book of Common Prayer has been banished to one early morning Communion service each month and they feel that liturgy has virtually disappeared. The music group leads most of the service with off-the-cuff contributions from whoever 'feels led'. There are times for open prayer, with prophetic contributions from the congregation. The music group encourages everyone to speak out in tongues, prayer or prophecy – all at the same time. The sermon seems to come as an afterthought. Holy Communion is celebrated very informally with the bread and wine being passed around. Some of the 'traditionalists' now only attend the 8 a.m. service where things are a little more formal – but having a woman celebrating may be the last straw for them!

ROLE PLAY the discussion between the vicar and the three or four members of the 'traditionalist' group.

Or discuss issues underlying the changing worship at St Saviour's? Why has it changed?

BIBLE STUDY

Read 11:17-22 and 14.23

Bible Link What concerned Paul about the impact the worship in Corinth had on the members of the church and on those who came from outside the church?

Respect Read 11:2-16

- What is Paul concerned about when he insists women should cover their hair when they pray or prophesy? How might such principles be worked out today?

Reverence Read 11:17-34

- Why did the behaviour in the worship at Corinth upset Paul? What attitude is Paul encouraging instead?

Upbuilding Read 14:20-32

- In what ways can our worship hinder those who attend? How can it help them?

Order Read 14:33-40

- How were the women affecting the worship in Corinth? How might the principle of verse 40 determine what happens in worship?

APPLICATION

How might the guidance given by these passages help shape worship today so that it is helpful both to Christians and outsiders? Are there lessons for your church to learn?

BEGIN HERE ALTERNATIVE

Think about your church's worship and complete the sentence 'I wish they wouldn't ...' What things annoy us about the way the church worships together?

ADDITIONAL QUESTIONS

Bible Link

How do divisions between Christians affect the worship of the church?

What sort of impact do different styles of worship have on outsiders who attend our services?

Respect

- What were women trying to say by flouting the customs of church and society? What was wrong with that?
- What do these verses teach about the interdependence of men and women?

Reverence

- How can we demonstrate an appropriate awe as we come to receive Holy Communion?

Upbuilding

- If our worship is to help those who are not yet Christians (14:22-25) how will that affect what we do? Does this create conflict with the expectations of those who are already Christians?
- In the context of church life today how can scope be found for the sort of involvement of every member in worship described in 14:26?
- Why is it important for individuals to submit their own Spirit-prompted words to the judgement of the wider church? Why do we not just accept what anyone contributes?

Order

- Why should we accept the general consensus of opinion in the life of the church (11:16 and 14:36-38)?
- How do the rules of your denomination shape the worship of your church?

WORSHIP & PRAYER

The Holy Communion Service has been a focus of this week's study. Use prayers drawn from it in your worship this week, such as the opening prayer ('Almighty God, to whom all hearts'); the responses and thanksgiving leading to 'Holy, holy, holy'; the acclamation 'Christ has died; Christ is risen; Christ will come again'; the words at the breaking of the bread and the final prayers. These, together with songs from the list below, will enable the group to express various aspects of worship. Include prayer for those who lead the church's worship.

34	Angel voices ever singing	414	Let us break bread together
66	Broken for me	444	Lord, speak to me
92	Come, let us praise the Lord	462	May the fragrance of Jesus
131	Father God, we worship you	721	We break this bread
214	He gave His life in selfless love	723	We come as guests invited
238	Holy, holy	729	We have come into his house

7 All Good Gifts
1 CORINTHIANS 12:1 - 14:19

AIM To discover how to use our gifts for the good of all.

INTRODUCTION

In recent years many Christians have discovered anew the tremendous variety of spiritual gifts described by Paul in passages such as this. Now, as then, that has led to divisions in the church. Some will want to play down the role of some of these gifts. Others will be really excited about new things God has done in their lives and the gifts they have received. Some will feel that their gifts should give them a prominent place in church life. Others will feel their gifts are insignificant or non-existent and that they have no effective part to play in the life of the church. It can all become very divisive. We need to learn that all gifts are given by the same Holy Spirit, that the church is one, that love matters more than gifts and that we need to achieve a proper perspective on the gifts we have. God's gifts are not to be despised, but, more importantly, neither are any of God's people!

BIBLE NOTES

12:1-3 The Christians in Corinth have asked Paul questions about using spiritual gifts. It would seem that gifts such as prophecy were used with great enthusiasm but some people while 'inspired' were saying 'Jesus is cursed'. Paul says such a confession is a sign of demonic inspiration like that experienced in the worship of idols. Confessing Jesus as Lord is a sign that the Holy Spirit is at work in a person.

12:4-6 These verses stress that all gifts have the same source – God. Three Greek words are used to describe the gifts – they are *charismata* – gifts of grace (*charis*) freely given; *diakonia* – ways of serving; *energemata* – ways in which God's power is at work. There is a reference to the Trinity here too as Paul speaks of Spirit, Lord (that is Jesus) and God (that is the Father).

12:7-11 These verses stress that different gifts are given to different people but they are given for the good not of the individual but of the whole church. It is hard to be precise about the nature of some of these gifts. The difference between a 'word of wisdom' and a 'word of knowledge' is not clear. Both are gifts of speaking. Wisdom may refer to an understanding of God and his ways and how we are called to live; while knowledge may be insight into particular situations or personal needs. Faith is the ability to trust God to provide or work in particular situations. It has links with gifts of healings (plural in the original Greek, suggesting God acting in different ways to meet particular needs) and miracles which must be signs of God's power at work in ways other than in healing. Prophecy includes speaking about future events (see Acts 11:27-30 and 21:8-14) but also seems to refer to the more general speaking of a message inspired by the Holy Spirit to build up, encourage or console (see 14:3). The insight to distinguish between spirits enables us to know whether something is inspired by God or not. In Acts 2 the gift of tongues was the ability to speak in other languages understood by those listening. Here it appears to be speaking to God with words the speaker does not understand. In a meeting some have the ability to interpret or explain what has been spoken in tongues.

12:12-13 Paul begins here to use the body as a description of the Church in its unity. By baptism we are brought into oneness with Christ and so into oneness with his body, the Church. Baptism is not just an outward symbol, it is linked with receiving the Holy Spirit inwardly (pictured in terms of 'drinking').

12:14-26 The humorous analogies here clearly make the point that everyone with their gifts, however insignificant they seem, is important in the church.

12:27-30 Paul lists a number of gifts here, some of which were mentioned in verses 7-11 (see the commentary on those verses). But the emphasis here is more on gifted people than on the gifts. There are those who exercise gifts not from time to time but as a regular part of their ministry. Apostles are those who have seen the risen Christ and have been specially called by him to leadership in the church. Teachers instruct the church. Helpers are probably those who help the poor and sick (perhaps the deacons). Administrators are those who help direct the church (perhaps its elders). Not everyone exercises all these gifts.

12:31-13:3 If Christians want gifts Paul encourages them to desire the most useful ones, but above all to follow the path of loving each other. This is to be the motive behind all we do. Without it all gifts are useless. We may even give away all we have or be burned as a martyr, but without love such actions are of no value.

13:4-7 Here we see love's characteristics described in terms of response to others.

13:8-13 Spiritual gifts are for here and now. They will not be needed in heaven when a full knowledge of God takes their place – just as adult understanding replaces the childish or perfect sight replaces the imperfect image seen in the metal mirrors used in Paul's day. Faith, hope and love endure. Faith and hope find their fulfilment in heaven when we see God, the object of our faith and our hope. Love is transferred to heaven – the relationship of love we have with God and with his people will be at the heart of the life in heaven. Love is the greatest of the three because it is God's very own nature.

14:1-5 Having put love at the heart of all we do, Paul harks back to his words in 12:31 and goes on to give guidelines about the gifts of tongues and prophecy. Tongues help the individual but only help the church if someone interprets. Prophecy strengthens the church.

14:6-12 Paul uses various pictures to show that the gift of tongues by itself used in public is just an unhelpful noise. Other gifts are more helpful – 'revelation' (which may be the same as the 'word of wisdom' in 12:8), knowledge, prophecy and teaching.

14:13-19 If we have the gift of tongues and want to use it in public we should pray for the gift of interpretation too. The gift of tongues enables our inward spirit to pray, expressing, maybe, feelings which we cannot put into words. It is a good gift but it bypasses the mind. We need to pray and sing with the mind in our own language, as well as in tongues. In church others cannot join in our prayer in tongues, a few words in ordinary speech are far more useful.

SUNDAY EXTRA
Use today's sermon to teach about spiritual gifts and their **1. Character** (12:2-3) **2. Unity** (12:4-6) **3. Purpose** (12:7) **4. Nature** (12:8-10) **5. Source** (12:11).

Alternatively emphasise the unity of the body by talking about **1. One body – many parts 2. One Spirit – many gifts.**

For All-age worship use a drawing of a body cut up as a jigsaw. Get help to put it together – but have one vital piece, such as the feet, hidden to be searched for by the congregation. Emphasise that the body cannot get anywhere without all the parts and talk about the parallels with church life.

You could develop a sketch of the argument between various parts of the body. Pray for the local church and its unity, for the valuing of all its members and the use of their gifts.

7

Group Sheet

All Good Gifts

1 CORINTHIANS 12:1 - 14:19

AIM To discover how to use our gifts for the good of all.

CASE STUDY

Division is breaking out again at St Saviour's. After his meeting with the traditionalist lobby, the vicar has been trying to discourage over-frequent use of the gifts of tongues and prophecy in the services. He now leads much of the worship himself and has been insisting that one of his roles is to exercise the gift of discernment in deciding what is a right contribution to worship and what is not. He has met with a very angry response from the members of the Johnsons' house group. They feel that the church is losing the 'freedom in the Lord' that it had and is showing contempt for gifts which everyone should be encouraged to exercise. They want to see the music group (several of whom belong to the house group) back in charge of the worship – after all, they are far more gifted in this area than Graham! Some of the house group are also unhappy because Graham is allocating more time to preaching. One or two of them had also been feeling that they had a special gift of healing and had been in discussion with Graham about ways their gifts could be used in healing services. They think he has had second thoughts. Some very unkind things have been said about the way Graham has been seeking to exercise authority in leading the church. 'We don't need that sort of leadership when the Spirit is in control,' they argue. 'If the traditional lot don't like what God has been doing at St Saviour's they can go out to one of the villages like Milton-in-the-Marsh – they've all got cars. If they were really born-again Christians they would know that what is happening is God's will.'

ROLE PLAY the meeting when the vicar visits Philip and Maureen Johnson's house group.

Or discuss reasons why the use of gifts has become such a divisive issue at St Saviour's. Why are the members of the Johnson's house group keen to develop the use of gifts?

BIBLE STUDY

Read 12:16-17, 21

Bible Link What sorts of division can be caused by an emphasis on gifts?

One Spirit Read 12:1-13

● How can the variety of gifts be seen as a cause of unity rather than division?

One Body Read 12:14-31

● Why are all people with all of their gifts needed? How can we ensure that everyone is valued?

Loving
Read 13:1-13

● How does the emphasis upon love affect the way we exercise spiritual gifts?

Edifying
Read 14:1-19

● How will the need to build up the church shape our attitudes to the various gifts of the Spirit and the way we use them?

APPLICATION

How does the teaching of this passage help us to keep the role of gifts in a proper perspective? How can we encourage a right use of the gifts God has given to his people?

BEGIN HERE ALTERNATIVE

If you could have one extra gift to help you play a better part in the life of the church, what would it be and why? How do you feel about the gifts you have?

ADDITIONAL QUESTIONS

Bible Link Why can humility and pride both lead to a wrong evaluation of the gifts God has given us?

One Spirit

- What understanding do you have of the character of the gifts listed in 12:8-10 and 28?
- What do we learn here about the way the Holy Spirit is at work in the Church?

One Body

- How do the principles in 12:26 work out in practice? How can we show care for one another?

Loving

- How would the sort of love described in 13:4-7 help to resolve differences in the life of the church? (You might like to look at each description in turn to see how that response would shape our reactions and our behaviour towards other people.)
- Why are faith, hope and love more important than spiritual gifts?

Edifying

- What does Paul see as a right use of the gift of tongues?
- How do we gauge whether something is positively upbuilding or not?

WORSHIP & PRAYER

We need to appreciate the gifts God has given us. Ask everyone to think of one gift God has given to the person sitting on their right and to give thanks for that gift. Use all or part of 1 Corinthians 13 as a meditation or turn the middle section into a prayer ('Help us to show love which is patient ...'). Pray for those who lead the church and for the use of all the gifts God has given us.

18	All over the world	427	Lord, come and heal your church
38	As we are gathered	442	Lord of the church
54	Bind us together	532	Oh! Oh! Oh! how good is the Lord
198	Gracious Spirit, Holy Ghost	611	Spirit of holiness
241	Holy Spirit, we welcome you	650	The King is among us
367	Jesus is Lord	771	Wind, wind blow on me

7

Faithful to the End

1 CORINTHIANS 15 & 16

AIM To see how Christian beliefs shape Christian lives.

INTRODUCTION

Death is currently a taboo subject in Western society. We prefer to imagine that it only happens to people outside the circle of our family and friends. That, of course, is a delusion and from time to time we are confronted with the reality of death and have to think about it. Growing numbers feel that death is the end. There is no eternal life. Others feel the human spirit must live on but are drawn to ideas such as reincarnation.

The Christian hope of life after death is based on the fact of Christ's resurrection. Without that, says Paul, we have no grounds for hope. His resurrection is the pattern for ours and so we believe not in the survival of the soul beyond death but in the resurrection of the body. Our bodies are an essential part of us; they enable us to express what is in our hearts and minds. Our future hope helps us keep the present in perspective. It enables us to keep living and working for God. The gospel message of Christ's death and resurrection is essential not just for the future but for life now.

BIBLE NOTES

15:1-2 There were those in Corinth who were in some way denying the resurrection of the dead. They may have followed Greek philosophy in believing in the immortality of the soul and despising any idea of the resurrection of frail, sinful bodies. They may have believed that there was no future resurrection because we have already been 'raised with Christ', experiencing new life now (like Hymenaeus and Philetus in 2 Timothy 2:17). Paul brings them back to the facts of the gospel he preached. It is this gospel by which they are being saved. (The original Greek suggests an ongoing process of salvation.) They must hold fast to this message, not to do so would be to betray their original belief.

15:3-4 This is not just Paul's message but the common Christian tradition. It is a fulfilment of Old Testament prophecy in passages such as Isaiah 53, which speak of the Messiah's death. Isaiah 53:10-12 also suggests his resurrection. The insistence that Christ was buried is a vital link – it emphasises that he really was dead and that he actually rose from the dead.

15:5-7 Paul is not afraid to refer them to a host of witnesses to Christ's resurrection. We read about the appearances to Peter (Cephas) in Luke 24:34 and to the twelve in Luke 24:36 and John 20:19; 'the five hundred' may refer to an appearance in Galilee (Matthew 28:7). There is no record of an appearance to James but what else would explain the transformation of a sceptical brother into the leader of the church in Jerusalem? He was already part of the group who met after Christ's ascension (Acts 1:14). The final reference to an appearance to the apostles is probably to Christ's meeting with them before his ascension (Acts 1:6-11).

15:8-11 Paul includes himself in the list, even though his encounter did not happen at the 'right' time. God's grace touched even the church's fiercest persecutor and turned him into its foremost preacher.

15:12-20 Paul lists the consequences of denying the idea of resurrection – the first of which is that Christ cannot have been raised. All else depends on that – Paul's preaching, their faith, forgiveness and future hope. But Christ has been raised, a token for them of their resurrection, just as the first fruits gathered are a token of the full harvest to come.

15:21-22 Paul here and in verses 45-50 speaks of humanity linked to Adam and sharing the death he brought into the world. But through another man, Christ, there is a new humanity and those linked to him are raised to life.

15:23-28 Christ's resurrection comes first. Ours comes when he returns. Then follows the completion of God's plan for a rebellious world when all is brought into perfect submission and harmony. Verse 25 quotes Psalm 110:1. Verse 2 quotes Psalm 8:6 – Christ fulfills God's vision for humanity found there. Christ is subject to God not because of any inequality in his divine nature but because his work as Saviour is completed and sovereignty is handed back to God when everything is in perfect order.

15:29 It is not certain what this practice was – possibly a reference to a proxy baptism for Christians who died suddenly before they were baptized. This would be pointless if there was no resurrection.

15:30-34 Paul's efforts and the opposition he endured were of no use if there was no resurrection – why not have a good time instead?

15:35-41 To those who found it hard to envisage our disfigured human bodies being raised, Paul points out that the resurrection body will be a real body but with a different character. These illustrations show that even now such an idea is familiar. Seed and plant flow from each other but are different. There are different sorts of flesh – as we experience when we eat meat, birds or fish. Earth, moon, sun, stars are all heavenly bodies but have different sorts of glory.

15:42-57 These verses contrast what it means to belong to the first Adam, created out of dust and returning to dust (Genesis 2:7 and 3:19) and what it means to belong to Christ, 'the last Adam'. Our physical, mortal bodies are instantly transformed into imperishable, immortal bodies when the trumpet sounds to announce Christ's return in glory (see 1 Thessalonians 4:13-18). Christ's victory over death can then be celebrated in fulfilment of the Old Testament. Verse 54 quotes Isaiah 25:8 and verse 55 quotes Hosea 13:14. It is sin which gives death its sting because death is the punishment for sin. The Law gives sin its power by condemning us as sinners (Romans 7:7-14), but Christ has dealt with sin and death and we share in his victory.

15:58 With a secure hope for the future our work for God will not be in vain.

16:1-4 Paul was organising support for the poor members of the church in Jerusalem (see Galatians 2:9-10 and 2 Corinthians 9:1-5).

16:5-20 These verses reflect the comings and goings of Paul and his fellow Christians and the mutual support of one group for another. Timothy (16:10) was one of Paul's closest companions (see Acts 16:1-3, Colossians 2:19-24 and 1 and 2 Timothy). On Apollos see notes on 1:12 and for Stephanus, Fortunatus and Achaicus, Aquila and Prisca (Priscilla) see **Introducing 1 Corinthians.**

16:21-24 Paul usually authenticates his letters by writing the final section himself. The other verses here reflect phrases used in worship, including the prayer 'Our Lord, come', which like 'Amen' is not a Greek word but Aramaic, reflecting its very early origins in the church in Palestine.

 SUNDAY EXTRA
The major theme this week is the difference Christ's resurrection makes. You could focus on 15:12-20 and point out all that depends on Christ rising from the dead – **1. Our preaching (forthtelling!)** (15:14-15) **2. Our faith** (15:17) **3. Our forgiveness** (15:17) **4. Our future hope** (15:18-19). Or you could use the second half of the chapter to talk about the consequences of **1. Adam's disobedience   2. Christ's obedience.**

In a Family Service you might like to 'interview' some of the witnesses to Christ's resurrection or use drawings of Peter, James and Paul and talk about how meeting the risen Christ changed their lives. Interview some of the congregation to discover what knowing the risen Christ means to them. In the prayers give thanks for Christ's resurrection and its impact on us. Pray for those who are dying and those who have not discovered the truth of the resurrection message.

Group Sheet

8

Faithful to the End
1 CORINTHIANS 15 & 16

AIM To see how Christian beliefs shape Christian lives.

CASE STUDY

Dave Morgan, St Saviour's church warden, is attending the funeral of his Great Aunt Dora. At the meal following the service he has been hearing some intriguing comments about death, quite a few of them from church members. His down-to-earth Uncle Fred says, 'I don't know what all the fuss is about. When you're gone, you're gone. Why bother with the church and all this resurrection nonsense? Dead men don't rise – that's all there is to it.' Fred's wife Alice is not so sure: 'What about all those people who say they have come back from the dead, and those who say they have been someone else in a previous life. I like that idea of coming back again and being given another chance.' One of the church members, Debbie Walker, responded: 'I don't think it really matters whether Jesus rose again. I think that Bishop was right. It's our experience of Christ's 'risenness' transcending death which matters.' Her husband Steve adds, 'I'm not really sure what, if anything, happens after death, but having new life in Jesus makes a real difference to life here and now.' When Dave tried to talk about eternal life only being possible through Christ, someone said: 'If God is love, everyone will be OK in the end.'

ROLE PLAY the conversation after Great Aunt Dora's funeral.

Or discuss the variety of views about death expressed in the comments after the funeral and in the views of people you know.
How do people cope with the fact of death?

BIBLE STUDY
Read 15:12-13 and 35
Bible Link What sorts of questions did Christians in Corinth have about the resurrection?

Facts Read 15:1-19
- What evidence does Paul give for the resurrection of Christ? Why does he think it is important to believe that Christ has been raised?

First Fruits Read 15:20-28
- What do these verses show about the impact of Christ's victory over death?

Future Read 15:35-56
- What does Paul teach here about the transformation of our physical bodies at Christ's return?

Faithfulness Read 15:58-16:24
- How do the examples of service in Chapter 16 illustrate what it means to obey the instructions about faithful service given in 15:58? What equivalents might there be in life today?

APPLICATION
How does our view of the meaning and consequences of Christ's death and resurrection shape the way we live life now? Why do we need to hold on to those beliefs firmly?

BEGIN HERE ALTERNATIVE

Complete the sentence 'Death is....' What do our statements say about our feelings concerning death?

ADDITIONAL QUESTIONS

Bible Link

What encourages people to drift away from a straightforward faith in Christ's death and resurrection?

Facts

- What does Paul mean when he says Christ died and rose again 'according to the Scriptures'? Why do you think he felt it important to emphasise that?
- What arguments against the resurrection of Christ do people use? How are they answered in this passage?

First Fruits

- What does Paul say here about the completeness of everything at the end of time?

Future

- How does Christ's identification with us as the 'last Adam' bring about our hope of eternal life?
- What encouragement do you get from Paul's picture of the transformation of our bodies?
- Why does Paul emphasise the resurrection of the body, rather than the immortality of the soul or other 'alternative' ideas about life after death?

Faithfulness

- Why does our future hope encourage steadfastness now?

WORSHIP & PRAYER

This week's study gives us an opportunity to celebrate all Christ has done for us in dying and rising again. Sing or say together songs which rejoice in those facts, such as 'These are the facts' (*Mission Praise* 687) or say one of the Creeds or the canticle Te Deum together. Pray for those facing death and those who mourn and for the church's proclamation of the gospel message. Some suitable songs from *Mission Praise* are listed below.

14	All heaven declares	340	In the tomb so cold
74	Christ is risen! hallelujah!	358	Jesus Christ is alive today
155	For this purpose	601	Sing alleluia to the Lord
219	He that is in us	670	The strife is o'er
220	He is Lord	687	These are the facts
266	I cannot tell	691	This is the day

CPAS is an Anglican mission agency helping churches to evangelise, teach and pastor. Our staff work across Great Britain and Ireland to bring our fourfold mission of support to the local church and its leaders.

EVANGELISM

We help church members, both ordained and lay, to become more effective in their individual and corporate Christian witness. We offer a complete service for local church needs, from parish assessment work to preparations for missions, from adult training in personal evangelism to training in children's evangelism, from mission strategy for the local church to reaching the unchurched. Training is tailored to the practical needs and realities of the community in which the church lives.

LOCAL CHURCH LEADERSHIP

We help clergy and laity in their leadership roles. We do this by running training courses on a wide range of topics and by providing help and advice about specific parish situations. We publish an extensive catalogue of resources to help local church leaders and regular mailings tailored to the need of clergy *(Church Leadership Pack)*, Readers and youth and children's leaders *(CYFA Leaders' Newspaper, Pathfinder Pack and Children in Churches)*. We have a special programme, called Ministry Among Women, to help women discover their potential as leaders and to resource them in that role.

We nominate incumbents to over 500 parishes, making us the largest Patron in the Church of England after the Crown, and we make substantial grants each year to help churches pay for additional people to work with existing church leaders, especially in inner city areas. Our Vocation and Ministry Division run *You & the Ministry* weekends for those contemplating full time ministry. *CPAS Readers* gives the opportunity for meeting and learning with other Readers and finding out what other churches are doing, through conferences and publications.

YOUNG PEOPLE, CHILDREN AND FAMILIES

We provide biblical teaching, resources and training for the leaders of CYPECS groups *(CYFA, Pathfinders, Explorers, Climbers and Scramblers)* for young people and children in local churches. Each year over 10,000 children, young people and leaders attend camps and houseparties. Our *Ministry Among Women* unit also supports work among *Families and Under Fives*, helping churches to reach out into their communities in service and evangelism.

PUBLICATIONS

We are a major publisher of Christian resource materials, from workbooks to major video-based training courses for local church use on important themes of Christian ministry such as Christian discipleship and marriage. All our publications are subsidized to help churches afford them. Increasingly non-Anglican as well as Anglican churches and individuals are using our publications.

THE FUTURE OF CPAS

Our vision is to develop increasingly as a quality mission agency for the building up of local church ministry. We affirm the supremacy of Scripture in all our work. We are funded almost entirely by voluntary donations from individual supporters and churches.